The Paths Her Heart Has Journeyed

A compilation of my mother's poetry!

Terri Grant

Copyright © 2018 Terri Grant

All rights reserved. No part of this publication may be reproduced, distributed, or transmitted in any form or by any means, including photocopying, recording, or other electronic or mechanical methods, without the prior written permission of the publisher, except in the case of brief quotations embodied in critical reviews and certain other noncommercial uses permitted by copyright law.

ISBN: 978-1-7326934-3-2

Liberation's Publishing LLC
West Point, Mississippi
www.liberationspublishing.com

From the Writer's Heart.

I hope no one will be misguided by any of my work. I believe in "God" and I do not condone sin in any way. Sin is never acceptable by "God". I am a writer! I am inspired by "God" to do inspirational writing. I also write from my heart sometimes about life as I have lived it. I write about love, despair, death, and joys of life.

Alice Thompson pen named Olivia Dupree

From the Daughter's heart.

My beautiful mother, Alice Thompson, published a series of poetry throughout her life under her pen name Olivia Dupree. Her books include "A Journey of the Heart" and "Inspirations of the Heart". Her writing is beautiful and full of meaning. My mother, Alice, is alive and well, and republishing her work is my way of keeping her legacy here well after she has gone own to bless heaven with her presence. It is her flowers before her while she lives.

God bless you enjoy!
Terri

Terri Grant

Table of Content

Grow Old With Me 7

Images of a Child 8

Wonders of the Heart 9

A Poet 10

Magic 11

As Much 12

At Last 13

My Love 14

Vision of a Dream 15

Sins of the Heart 16

Something About My Love 17

Amazing Grace, Blues, and Jazz 18

The Other Side of Midnight 19

The Blues 20

Before Dawn 21

Darkness and Light 22

Tell a Riddle, Tell a Story 23

Let Me Tell You 24

Now I Know 25

An Angel In My Heart 26

The Bible 28

A Place Called Heaven 29

A Blessed Soul 30

Things to be Done 31

Say Goodbye to Yesterday 32

Beside Still Waters 33

Time Alone 34

Home 35

Magic 36

My Friend 37

In the Midst of a Storm 38

Happy New Year 39

Grow Old With Me

Grow old with me
Grow old with me, age in grace and
Together we will find comfort in knowing
There's still much to be discovered.

Grow old with me through our golden years and
Together we will age in love. Remembering
Day of youth. "Yet aged in grace, in a time
When friendship embrace passion and
Surrender too unforgettable memories
To be shared in the heart."

Come grow old with e and the desires of our
Heart will reach beyond heights and depths of our soul.
Grow old with me and find silent pleasure
In knowing we are still together.

Stay with me in days of young, and if by chance
Fate grant in and we are still in love in our rockin'
The way we were. Grow old with me, and
Discover love in a quiet kind of way.
Come grow old with me.

Images of a Child

7-14-1993

In a crowd, I glimpse an image of a
Small child that could have been you.
As the days go by, I count the years,
And wonder about a child

I see an image of you in the faces of
Children of all ages. I hear cries from
An empty crib, and long to sing,
"Hush little baby don't you cry."

I see an image of you held in the arms of
A stranger. I wonder about the child I never
Knew, but in a very unique way, I was
Touched by a little angel I will always
Hold dear to heart.

Images of a child.
My child, my sweet angel,
"Good night my darling."

Wonders of the Heart

Quiet moments of silence
On a cool autumn morning,
A breeze of romance showers my soul.
As love blooms, my heart wonders
How long will you love me,
How long will we be together.

Mysteries of the mind explore my soul,
As love searches for a place in eternity.
My heart wonders how long will you stay,
How long will I love you,
My heart silently whispers,
"I will love thee for the rest of my life."

Wonders of the heart, wonders of my heart.
Where answers lie in the depth of the heart.
Wonders of the heart, wonders of my heart.
How long will you love me?

A Poet

A poet may wonder about the unknown,
Glimpse Heaven from a distance hill,
Find inspiration in green pastures
Beside still waters and serenity
In the shadows of death.

A poet may take for inspiration what is
Seen through the eyes of a child,
Then hurry home and
Write about life

Through the heart of a poet, whispered
Word are heard, and silent pain
Comforted by the mystery
That lies in the heart
And soul of a poet.

Inspiration inspired by "God". A poet rises
With dawn, and writes until night falls,
Of things unseen, still longed for.

Out of poet's heart, flows wisdom.
Listen quietly, and a poet will tell
You something about yourself.
A poet.

Magic

The earth is full of magic
Magic is the birth of a child as aging approaches,
The calmness of the sea after a raging storm,
The sign of the rainbow after a spring shower.
Magic is wondering where light rest
When darkness covers the earth.

Magic: how seasons begin and end
In their own time reason.
Magic in the melody of hummingbird.
As a willow tree weeps on a hill.
Magic in the twinkling of stars on a clear night,
Yet the most unique magic is
When one falls in love.
Love is Magic.

As Much

12-31-1999

Never in my life have I ever loved as much,
Until too many years past.

Since then odd places are now familiar,
And on the other side of town
I bury my morals along with my guilt.
Never have I loved as much,
Before years long past.

On the eve of a new year,
"here we are till together,"
Tomorrow I hope to see you again,
For I can't say good-bye, not now,
And when say good-bye,
I will surely know, never in my life,
Have I ever loved as much.

At Last

A love like mine only comes once in a lifetime.
Looking beyond my broken past,
In my heart you've planted seeds of joy,
My soul reaped the harvest and
Together we discover my heart.

In every waking moment through your love
My passion for life look beyond ending,
I will love you as long as l live.
Years past beyond yesterday's seasons,
And still I dream of years to come.
Remembering days of long ago,
"here in a time where my dreams are
Beyond reality, a love like mine
Only comes once in a lifetime,
My true love has come along at last."

My Love

My darling, my love, I will always love you. When
I am absent from you, my heart and soul is in
Harmony, my heart embrace my soul and
I feel your presence.

My dearest darling, you laugh with me and when I
Am sad, your charm warms my heart. When I cry
You are there before the last tear drop falls.
When my burdens are heavy, I find silent
Meaning in your arms. You are my
Strength and my shelter in the storms of life.

My love my darling, you are my sweet inspiration,
And when you make love to me you touch
My inner mysteries and my fantasies
Reached beyond boundaries.

My darling my love, you are my only love. Where
Ever I am, in my heart you will always be.
I will love you the rest of my life,
My love.

Vision of a Dream

Follow me in my dream fulfilled
The desires of my Heart,
And I will love you through the night.
Hold me tight, hold me close and maybe
Tomorrow I will still be in your arms,
Then we will say good bye.

Night draws near, my soul rest
on the other side of dawn,
in a world where you always stay the night,
hold me close hold me tight,
and maybe you will stay
the whole night through.

Echoes of whispering wind like
Soft sweet kisses stir my soul,
Visions fade and I awake
From out of a dream, and waves
Of heat warm empty bed.
Hold me tight, hold me
Close and maybe tomorrow I will still be
In your arms and you will follow me
In my dreams and stay one more night.
I wonder did you stay the night,
Or was it just a vision of a dream?

Sins of the Heart

I lose sight of what is before me,
And bury my sins in silence.

A soul in need of redemption
Stands on a grave of hell.
My own sin cause a rage in the heart
And war within my soul.

In quiet moments of thought fear comes upon me,
Knowing it is promised my sins
Will soon come to light.

Dark as my path may seem, to free my soul,
I must free my heart, and loose the chains
That bind me. A heart free of sin
Is at peace with the soul.

Something About My Love

There is something about my love that makes me
Sad and when my love holds me close,
My Heart is made glad. My heart wanders far
From home, my path become bitter sweet,
And my journey back home is long.
My morals I put aside and accept
What is not rightfully mine,
"There is something about my love."

Night brings no rest in a bed of solitude, lying
Guilty I think about my love. Loneliness
Creeps in my heart and them I cry myself
To sleep. My guilt found in the arms of
My love, sacred vows broken, weaved
In a web of sin. My crime
Something about my love.

Honesty revealed when love is sowed in passion
And reaped painfully in the heart. I kneel
At the altar and ask forgiveness for
My sins, and in shame I hurry off to
Embrace my love. My sin lies in
Knowing the truth,
"There is something about my love."

Amazing Grace, Blues and Jazz

Some may say "Amazing Grace" Blues and Jazz
Have something in common,
As for "me", that is still yet to be seen.
The blues creates a rage in the heart
And disrupts the mind.

Jazz seems to calm the mind,
And create an illusion in the heart.
Don't sing me no blues, or play me no jazz,
Something about "Amazing Grace" that stir
My soul, and my heart rejoice in the "Lord".

Amazing Grace, Blues and Jazz:
The blues and jazz will cheat the heart,
And rob the soul.
Amazing Grace will reach beyond the heart,
And save a soul.

Don't sing me no blues, or play me no jazz
When my burden are heavy,
"I just have a little talk with Jesus".
And joy is found in the midst of sorrow.
When the blues come upon me,
'I sing a new song and hum a hymn of praise,
"Amazing Grace".

The Other Side of Midnight

12-31-1999

Somewhere my love waits in a place
Just beyond dawn, where comfort is found
In cold winter days, echoes of spring
Heard in the heart and hot summer nights,
Cooled by the intimacy of fall.

On the other side of midnight,
Together we create a world
Where only we exist,
And boundaries have no limits.

Just before dawn, you change my time,
Gave me a reason to look beyond midnight,
And see tomorrow.

"My love, the love of my life, my forbidden love.
How splendid knowing tomorrow my love waits on
The other side of midnight, for me."

The Blues

The blues I've had, blues I've heard,
A few sights I've seen that gave me the blues.
The pain in a hungry child's eyes,
And a homeless family striving for a dream,
As a generation destroys its own.
So don't sing me no sad song, blues I've heard.

The blues I've had after long, hot,
Passionate nights
In someone else's man's arms,
Then I sing the blues all week long, alone.
Blues I've heard, promises made kept,
A heart left broken accompanied by the blues.

The blues I've had, blues I've seen,
So don't sing me no sad song,
The blues I've heard all too well,
And I've been telling you
About the blues I've lived.

Before Dawn

12-31-1999

Before the early morning light of dawn
I will look within me, in search of answers
To questions I've dared not ask,
For fear I knew the answer.
I got a moon above me
And somebody who love me.
Star above me, a field of dreams and when the morning sun rises
It shines in my window.
I am not materially rich, but I am doing ok,
Yet I still long for something.
At the end of a long day, and just before dawn,
I awake still longing
Yet angels have watched over me all night long.

Saturday night out on the town
And church all day Sunday,
At the end of the week I find myself
Still longing "for something."
Today I tell myself
When the evening sun goes down
And tomorrow comes I will look within my heart
And if I am still longing, perhaps
Before dawn I will just say "yes lord."

Darkness and Light

Dark as the journey may seem
It is not upon one alone.
The darkness fall,
Without darkness in our lives there would be
No light of day.

On the edge of night darkness
Sing a fearful tune of things unseen,
Yet there is something magical
That lingers between night and day.
Without darkness there would be
No distant starts to brighten our path
And remind us of our journey
Beyond midnight.

There is no fear of darkness
When we realize there is
"one who will lead us out of darkness,
To a light that shine beyond sight."
"God" holds that light for
"He" is the light of the world.

Tell a Riddle, Tell a Story

Today I tell a story, yesterday I told a riddle.
Tell a riddle, tell a riddle of a child's cry.
Once told by a child.

Moments of Silence ,
Visions from a past chills my soul.
It seems so far away and long ago
In a land forgotten,
I remember a child just like you,
I hear your cries, my soul grips your pain.
You love much, trust all, and give what is asked,
Yet what silently received just don't seem right.

Friends are children of image , you tell
Them of a world filled with dragons and monsters.
They listen quietly,
But all the hear is a riddle told by
A child, so they soon fade away.

Someday a child will grow up,
Finding meaning in a world
Where healing and new beginning awaits.
Until someday comes
A child must cry out in a loud voice, and
Tell a riddle until someone hears a child's cry.
Tell a riddle, tell a story of a child's cry.

Let Me Tell You

I can't tell you what I want you to know,
Read between the lines, listen closely,
And hear my silent cry.
I can't tell you about my pain,
Or the frown behind my smile,
My long lost love and lovers to be.

I can't tell you about the sights I've seen,
The beauty I see in a rose,
Or my passion for life long overdue to be lived.
Read between the lines and
I will tell you words of wisdom,
Sweet to the ear, and nourishment to the soul.
Let me tell you.

I can't tell you what I want you to know,
The pain in my heart won't let me tell,
So give me a pen and some paper,
Read between the lines and I will tell you
Of a heart in search of silent words
Long to be spoken.
Let me tell you.

Now I Know

1994

Out of darkness, pieces of a dream
Are shadows from a past.
Ties that binds a soul in need to be free,
A soul trouble by a past yet unknown.
Now I know.

I look in the mirror, I see an image of a stranger.
I look closer, and I see my soul, and if I listen
Quietly, I hear a storm rage, within me.
When I cry, my tears are for me.
Now I know.

I glimpse Death from a far, and now I want to live.
Out of my heart flows unspoken words long
To be spoken, and whispered secrets
Silence by fear.

From out of darkness I emerge to say good bye
To a stranger within, at last a soul set free,
Calm like a quiet storm.

Through God and a very special love,
Today I know who I am, I am a survivor.
Now I know sometimes when I cry,
I cry tears of joy.
Now I know.

An Angel In My Heart

My memories of a friend who was sexually molested as a young girl inspired me to write three poems in this booklet. These poems reflect the experiences and triumph over a past that was devastating. I hope these poems will inspire you, as my friend Angel inspired me.

Angel and I grew up together both in loving Christian homes, yet her parents never knew of her unfortunate childhood experience. During the time of Angel's traumatic experiences, being a child myself, I didn't understand why sometimes this sweet little girl was so sad. Sometimes when Angel felt she couldn't cope with the fears and pain, she would say, "I wish I were an angel so I can fly away." That was a long time ago. Looking back now I believe God put Angel and me together to help each other. I've learned so much from her.

Sexual abuse is a terrible thing for a child to go through. Some survivors of sexual abuse never fully recover and for some it takes years, but you can recover. I am not saying it will be easy. With all the emotional feeling, it can be very traumatic, but you can be a true survivor. You just can't do it alone. Find someone you trust to talk to, get professional help, and remember through "God" you can overcome anything. Sexual abuse survivors can have a happy, productive life, and you can love and trust again. To free yourself, you must put the past behind you and then the healing will begin.

It has been a long time since I have seen Angel. Several

years ago she and her family moved somewhere up north and I never got to tell her goodbye. My memories of her are emotional and inspirational. No matter where I journey in life, Angel will always be in my heart. Remembering her now I get a feeling of contentment, knowing she finally found what she always longed for; love, happiness and peace. Today, through "God" and very special love, Angel is free and truly a survivor. Writing about Angel completes my healing and I can now say goodbye to an Angel.

The Bible

This is all I need, the Word. The Holy Bible has guided my life from childhood to adulthood. Holding my bible against my heart I remember generations past. Here in this book lies my family tree. God's Word bares records of things seen and unseen.

The Holy Book: I read in silence, and echoes of praise fill my empty heart. God's Word gives hope in a troubled world today, and dreams of a Promised Land.

The Bible, the Word of God; read it daily. Listen quietly, and God will gently speak to you. Those who abide in the Word of God shall be blessed with the presence of God, and a phenomenal inner feeling of peace.

The Word of God will lead you through the shadows of death, and guide a soul to a cross on a hill called Calvary. This book is all I need. Indeed, it's the most treasured bestseller. The Holy Bible: writers and authors. Great men inspired by God to write the Bible.

A Place Called Heaven

High above the clouds and far away, somewhere in the elements is a place called Heaven. In the stillness of the night, I close my eyes and vision a place called Heaven where angels fly high above the heavenly clouds. Streets are paved with gold, a river flows with milk and honey. The air has a sweet smell of honeysuckle. There is a field of white lilies, and gates with strings of white pearls, in a place called Heaven.

A soul leaves its earthly body, and no longer exists. A soul flies on the wing of an angel, through a pillow of blue and white clouds to a rest stop, for the soul of a Christian in a place called Paradise. I listen quietly to a heavenly choir singing a Zion Hymn, "Amazing Grace", for there is a place called Heaven.

Somewhere in the elements above the clouds, I vision a place where there is no darkness. There is a light, bright as the star of David. A light that guides a soul on the wings of an angel to a place called Heaven.

Once more, I close my eyes and see a soul on the wings of an angel. I hear a heavenly choir with voices of angels singing "Blessed Assurance", for there is a final resting place for the soul of a Christian. A place where God is in the midst, in a place called Heaven.

A Blessed Soul

Blessed is he who has divine grace, a joyful heart filled with love and peace in knowing he is blessed. Blessed is he without ill health and one who remembers to say "Thank You, Lord."

How blessed it is to have family and friends to share in the joys of life. Blessed is being content in knowing you are blessed. Count your blessings daily and remember, blessings counted will outweigh sorrows in life.

Blessed is a mother with child, as birth makes way for a new beginning and ending, as souls age in grace. Blessed is a wise man who speaks words of wisdom, and tells a fool to be thankful, for he is blessed.

Things to be Done

Yesterday is gone, tomorrow may never come, still there are things to be done. Whispered words to be spoken, sights to be seen, and songs unsung to be sung. Sadness exchanged for joy, tears wiped, and sins forgiven to be forgotten. Still there are things to be done.

Miles traveled, steps to be taken, a soul to be helped along the way. A kind word to be spoken, stories to tell, and secrets told to be kept. Lost souls to be found. So many things to be done and not enough time in a day.

Yesterday is gone, tomorrow may never be. Yet to come, the most beautiful words to be heard, the sweetest words to be spoken, "Well done, thou good and faithful servant. You've done well.

Say Goodbye to Yesterday

Let go of the past, open your heart to a new beginning. Let go of yesterday's grief and sorrow, and open your arms wide to the joys life holds today, for tomorrow is not promised.

Yesterday's grief and troubles are too heavy to carry today, find strength in things overcome, then in your heart you will find healing. We have tasted the bittersweet memories of yesterday, now it's time to let go.

Today it's hard to say good-bye to yesterday, yet if faith grants you tomorrow, then you say good-bye to yesterday.

Beside Still Waters

Beside still waters, there is no fear in the midst of death's shadow. On the banks of a river, a cool breeze calms my troubled soul, and my spirit is renewed beside still waters.

Through the valley of green pastures, my sold finds comfort in quiet serenity, accompanied by the presence of the Lord. I hear angels above my head, and a vison of a river called Jordan.

Lord, lead me to a river where I may drink and thirst no more. A place where precious memories linger, on the banks of a river. I vision a promised land, beside still waters.

Time Alone

Alone at last, in the quietness of solitude, we hear the voice of God and heed to his Word. Quiet sounds whisper gently.

Sweet hour of peace, hidden fears forgotten, strength found in weakness, and contentment in knowing what a little time alone can do.

Time alone trickles like sands of an hourglass. Sweet moments of silence, things forgotten, things remembered. Alone at last not a sound to be heard, what a joyful feeling, time alone

Home

A house filled with love, warmth, and comfort is what makes a house a home. In the heart of a home, there's always room for all. Home, a place where family and friends are always eager to return. To a traveler, a sign reads, "Welcome, a safe haven for all."

Home is where childhood begins and leads to adulthood, with memorable moments of rooms filled with endless years of memories of a place back home. No matter where you travel and stop to sleep, t it's the Queen's palace the bed you dream of is always back home.

Miles traveled between land and sea, is never too far from home. A heart always wanders back home, if by letter or telephone. It is always good to hear from home. Home sweet home, what a wonderful place to return, Home

Magic

The earth is full of magic. Magic is the birth of a child as aging approaches, the calmness of the sea after a raging storm, the sign of a rainbow after a spring shower. Magic is wandering where light rests when darkness covers the earth.

Magic, how seasons begin and end in their own time and reason. Magic in the melody of a hummingbird, as a willow tree weeps on a hill. Magic in the twinkling of stars on a clear night, yet the most unique magic is when one falls in love. Love is Magic.

My Friend

A friend like no other whose love and mercy reaches beyond my faults. In search of a path yet unknown, I draw near to thee. He leads me to thy thrown of grace, and my faith eliminates all doubts.

When I become weary, he gives me strength. I delight in his ways, and find in him a resting place.

He shields me from unseen danger. My enemies can do me no harm. I cling to faith, and he give me the victory to endure.

When my journey ends in my darkest hour, he will lead me safely to the other side, and my going will be peaceful sleep.

What a joy and honor it will be, being in the presence of one like no other. "Oh what a friend we have in Jesus!"

My Friend

In the Midst of a Storm

My path becomes dark, blinded by doubts. My faith shattered by fear. As the storms of life keep raging, god hears my silent cry, renews my faith, and calms "My Storm".

There is something about the sultry stillness, that lurks before a storm. Rain descending from heaven, flashing lightening roaring thunder, and rushing winds blow in a fury way. As the storms keep raging, God brightens my way, and my hopes are seen in a rainbow of colors in the sky.

As an infant, God carried me through a raging stor, place me on safe grounds, and the angel of the Lord watched over me.

Storms, and storms of life will keep raging, Yet, I will not fear, for I have been in a storm. God bestowed favor upon me, and "I love the Lord, for he heard my cry" . God is my anchor in the midst of a storm.

Happy New Year

Another year has passed, resolutions made to be kept. A new year and new beginning has been granted us. Time given to share with friends and loved ones. With each new year we say goodbye to the old and welcome the new. We take a silent moment to remember friends and family no longer here. Now that last year is part of forever, we know not how long we share this precious year.

All past things are gone and over. The clock of life slowly ticks as we must share the beautiful new year God has given us, find hope in today! Dream of next year!

Happy New Year!

www.ingramcontent.com/pod-product-compliance
Lightning Source LLC
Chambersburg PA
CBHW060508080526
44584CB00015B/1599